Animal Legends

Retold by
CAROL WATSON

Illustrated by
NICK PRICE

CONTENTS

Series Editor: Heather Amery

Reading Expert: Betty Root
Centre for the Teaching of Reading
University of Reading

Why Monkeys Live in the Trees

Long ago in the jungle there was an old gorilla called Nijina. He was king of all the animals for miles around.

Nijina had a beautiful daughter. All the animals wanted to marry her but she did not know who to choose.

One day Nijina was swinging through the trees when he saw something lying on the ground. It was a barrel.

He took off the lid and inside he found some strange coloured water. He tasted it. It was like drinking fire.

"I have an idea," Nijina said to himself. He took the barrel of fire water home and called all the other animals together.

All the animals pushed forward. Each one wanted to be the first to try drinking the strange water.

The elephant was so big he pushed his way to the front. "I'll drink this down in two gulps," he laughed.

"In this barrel is some special water," said Nijina. "The animal who can drink all of it may marry my beautiful daughter."

He put his trunk into the barrel. But before he had tasted it he jumped back, screaming and snorting.

"It stings!" he said, waving his trunk in the air. "No one can drink that." He rushed away feeling very angry.

3

The hippopotamus boasted, "I live half my life in the river and drink water all the time. I'll soon swallow the fire water." He took a big mouthful. Then he spat it out and ran to the river to wash away the taste.

Next came the warthog. "I'll have a try," he said. "I'm used to eating and drinking all sorts of things."

The hog drank some of the water. But then he jumped away from the barrel in disgust and ran off grunting.

The leopard came forward. "You fools are all far too ugly to marry," he said. "Look at my beautiful coat and graceful body!" He tried to drink from the barrel but even the smell of the water made him feel sick.

The leopard could not drink any of it. The animals laughed at him and he crawled away in shame. A tiny monkey jumped out of the crowd. "Please, Nijina," he said, "May I try to drink the water from the barrel?"

The old gorilla smiled. "Of course you may try," he said. "But you must drink it all, and all of it today."

"May I drink a little at a time and take rests between drinks?" asked the monkey. "Yes," replied the gorilla.

All the animals gathered round to watch the tiny monkey. They did not believe he could drink the water.

The monkey climbed on to the barrel and said, "I, Telinga, will drink all the water and marry Nijina's daughter."

5

He gulped down a large mouthful of fire water and ran off into the bushes for a rest.

A few minutes later the monkey popped out of the bushes again and drank from the barrel.

Just as before, he jumped down and disappeared into the jungle for a while.

No one knew that behind the bushes there was a tribe of monkeys, all exactly the same.

Each one of these monkeys took his turn to drink the strange-tasting water.

By the end of the day the barrel was empty. "Now I shall meet my bride," said Telinga.

He stood before the king of the gorillas. "This is my daughter," said Nijina. "You may marry her."

But suddenly the giraffe caught sight of all the monkeys hiding in the bushes. "What are you doing there?" he cried.

"Telinga has cheated," roared the animals. "His whole tribe has helped him to drink the fire water!" "Kill them!" screamed the leopard and the warthog.

The frightened monkeys jumped into the trees and swung out of reach. There they have lived ever since and are afraid when they come down to the ground.

7

The Crocodile and the Rabbits

A long time ago when all crocodiles lived on the land, there was one grumpy old crocodile who lived by a river.

He was lazy and lay in the sun all day. One morning a baby rabbit hopped along looking for some food.

"Hello," said the rabbit. "Go away," grunted the crocodile, "I'm trying to sleep." He shut his eyes.

The rabbit saw a bunch of tasty leaves near the crocodile's nose. He crept up to them and began to nibble.

"Get away from those leaves!" roared the crocodile. He snapped at the rabbit with his big, sharp teeth.

The little rabbit ran away as fast as he could. He did not stop running until he reached his burrow.

"I ate the crocodile's leaves and he tried to eat me," said the baby rabbit to his mother. "I only just escaped."

The mother rabbit was very angry. "That nasty old crocodile," she said. "He's greedy and grumpy. It's time we taught him a lesson." All the family had a meeting to decide what trick they could play on the crocodile.

9

Next day all the rabbits went out into the woods and they collected branches, twigs and dried leaves.

They put them into a large sack. When the sack was full they went off in search of the horrible crocodile.

"There he is by the river bank," whispered the baby rabbit. "He's asleep as usual." They crept over to him.

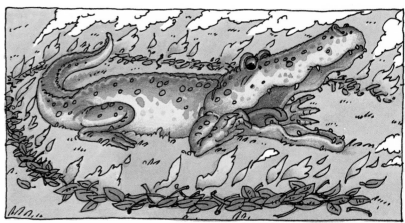

They put the branches, twigs and leaves in a large circle round the crocodile. He just went on snoring.

Then they did a very wicked thing. The mother rabbit set fire to the twigs and leaves. Soon the smoke

made the crocodile cough and the flames made him feel hot. Then he woke up. "Help! Fire!" he shouted.

He tried to run away but the fire was all around him. He leapt high into the air and jumped over the flames.

The crocodile ran to the river and dived in. The water soon cooled him down but he was still frightened.

Then he heard the rabbits squealing with laughter and he was very angry. "Don't you ever come near the river again," shouted the crocodile.

"And you keep away from our land," shouted the rabbits. From then on the crocodile always stayed near the river, and the rabbits lived in the fields.

11

How the Giraffe became a Giraffe

Long ago in Africa there lived a little brown antelope. He was very unhappy because he was not big and strong like the other animals. All he could do was run very fast so he always escaped from his enemies.

One day he saw a huge cheetah sitting on a rock. She was about to pounce on a man walking along below.

"I must warn him," thought the antelope. He ran past the man, flashing his short tail and snorting loudly.

The man turned and saw the cheetah. He shouted, threw his spear at her and she ran away. The man was safe.

"You saved my life, little antelope," said the man. "How can I thank you? What do you wish for most of all?"

"I wish I were big and strong," said the antelope. "I want to have horns and claws and a flapping tail."

"I am a witch doctor," said the man. "I'll see if my magic can help you." He lit a fire and cast a spell.

A few minutes later the antelope felt himself changing. His body grew larger and his short tail disappeared.

Two horns appeared on his head and he grew a long tail. It had a little brush on the end to flap the flies away.

The antelope was pleased with his new tail and he felt very fierce and brave with his new horns.

But when he was in danger he still had to run away, and his bigger body made him run much more slowly.

"I need longer legs to go with my bigger body," thought the antelope. He went to find the witch doctor.

The witch doctor listened to his problem. "I'll see what I can do," he said and cast another spell.

Suddenly the antelope's legs began to grow. They grew longer and longer until he was incredibly tall.

Then his neck began to grow as well. But as his neck grew longer, his horns became smaller and smaller.

14

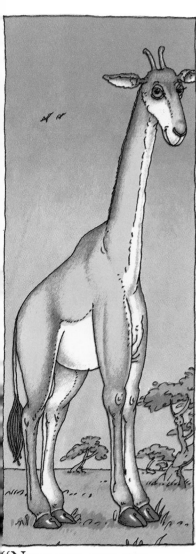

For a while the antelope was happy. With his long neck he could eat the juicy leaves from the tree tops. But his enemies could easily see his bright yellow neck amongst the shadowy trees. So he was still frightened.

"Now you can run faster," said the witch doctor. "And with your long neck you will see your enemies coming from far away."

He went again to the witch doctor and told him what was wrong. "Can I have patterns on my neck like a tree trunk?" he asked. "Then I shall be truly happy." The witch doctor was angry with the antelope.

15

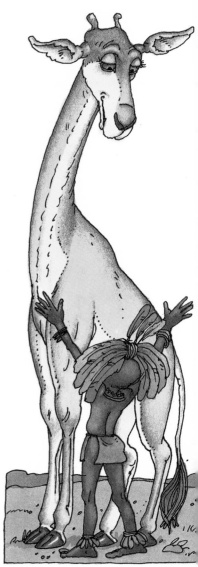

"You are never content," he said crossly. "You always want something more." He marched off to his hut.

"Wait here until morning," said the witch doctor. "Then I shall tell you what I have decided to do."

So the antelope waited all night outside the hut. The next day the witch doctor talked to him very firmly.

"This is the very last time I will do anything for you," he said. "You must not ask me for anything else."

He stood in front of the antelope and waved his arms in the air. Then he chanted some strange magic words.

Slowly the antelope changed and big, brown patches appeared on his skin. He tried to say "thank you" but he could not speak.

The witch doctor had cast a spell on the antelope's voice as well as his skin. He had made sure that he could never ask for anything more.

From then on he was called a giraffe. All giraffes are tall and graceful, but they are silent, and they will always be as timid as a little antelope.

17

The Cat and the Rat

Long ago the cat and the rat were good friends. They lived together on a desert island far away from anywhere. They did not have a care in the world and were very happy.

There were lots of tall trees for the cat to climb and fat birds for her to eat.

The rat ate juicy plants and roots. He dug holes and played in the sand all day.

One day the rat said "I'm bored with this island, let's go somewhere else."

"Good idea," replied the cat lazily, "but how are we going to get there?"

18

"Oh, that's easy," said the rat. "We'll make a boat from the trunk of a tree."

So the rat gnawed and nibbled at a tree with his sharp teeth until it fell down.

Then the cat scratched at the inside of the trunk to make a hollow for them to sit in.

They made two paddles from some branches, and at last they were ready to set off.

"All aboard!" cried the rat, "I hope I'm not going to get wet," said the cat.

"Of course not," the rat replied. He pushed the boat out and jumped in quickly.

They rowed and rowed until they were too tired to row any more. The cat fell asleep but the rat was hungry.

"We forgot to bring some food," he thought sadly. He was so hungry he began to nibble the side of the boat.

"What's that munching noise?" asked the cat sleepily. "Nothing," replied the rat. "You must be dreaming."

The cat went back to sleep and the rat went on nibbling. He nibbled so much he made a hole in the boat.

Suddenly water came in and the boat began to sink. The cat woke up. "I'm getting wet," she shouted.

She saw the hole in the boat. "We're sinking," she screamed. "I hope you can swim," cried the rat.

They swam for their lives towards the nearest shore. "This is your fault, you wicked rat," cried the cat.

"When we get to land I'm going to eat you up," she called. The rat swam even faster to the shore.

He ran to a sandhill and dug a hole. Then he disappeared into it so that the cat could not catch him.

The cat was very angry. "I'll wait for you here, rat," she said. "You will have to come out sometime."

But the rat dug a tunnel right through the hill and ran out the other side. The cat did not know and stayed there waiting to catch him.

From that day to this the cat always listens for the sound of a rat. She is still waiting for him to come out of his hole.

21

How the Turtle got its Shell

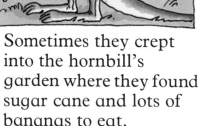

Once there were two friends, a turtle and a a wallaby. They went looking for food together every day.

Sometimes they crept into the hornbill's garden where they found sugar cane and lots of bananas to eat.

One day the hornbill had some of his friends round for a party. They wanted some sugar for their tea.

"I'll get some sugar cane from the garden," said the wagtail. "We can use that." She flew off to fetch it.

She saw the turtle and the wallaby eating the hornbill's bananas. "I must go and tell him at once," she thought.

She flew back. "The turtle and the wallaby are in your garden," she cried. "They are eating your food."

The birds were angry. They flocked together and flew off to the garden to catch the two animals.

The wallaby jumped over the fence when he saw the birds coming. But the poor turtle could not get away.

The birds swooped down and picked up the turtle. They carried her off into the kitchen and locked her in.

"Oh dear, what are they going to do to me?" thought the turtle. She was so frightened she hid under a bowl.

She stayed under the bowl and kept very still and quiet. When the birds came in they could not see her.

"The turtle has escaped," cried the hornbill. "We must find her." They all flew out of the room in a panic.

23

The turtle peeped out and saw the door was open. She crept out of the kitchen with the bowl still on her back.

As she hurried towards the beach the birds saw her. "Kill her!" they cried and they dropped stones on top of her.

But the stones bounced off the bowl and did not hurt the turtle at all. She dived into the sea and was safe.

From that time on wherever the turtle went she always kept the bowl on her back to protect her.